Inspection and

Forthcoming titles in the No-Nonsense series:

Steps in Leadership
Huw Thomas
1-84312-434-3

Managing People
Huw Thomas
1-84312-452-1

Inclusion
Linda Evans
1-84312-453-X

Managing Finance, Premises and Health & Safety
David Miller, John Plant & Paul Scaife
1-84312-454-8

Making the Most of Headship
1-84312-435-1

Inspection and Accountability

Bill Laar

 David Fulton Publishers

David Fulton Publishers Ltd
The Chiswick Centre, 414 Chiswick High Road, London W4 5TF

www.fultonpublishers.co.uk

First published in Great Britain in 2006 by David Fulton Publishers

10 9 8 7 6 5 4 3 2 1

David Fulton Publishers is a division of Granada Learning Limited.

Note: The right of Bill Laar to be identified as the author of this work
has been asserted by him in accordance with the Copyright, Designs
and Patents Act 1988.

British Library Cataloguing in Publication Data
A catalogue record for this book is available from the British Library.

ISBN: 1-84312-436-X

EAN: 978-1-84312-436-8

Typeset by RefineCatch Limited, Bungay, Suffolk
Printed and bound in Great Britain

Contents

Foreword *by Gerald Haigh*   vii

Introduction   1
1 The framework for inspecting schools   4
2 Self-evaluation   16
3 'Every Child Matters'   33
4 Spiritual, moral, social and cultural development   45
5 The Foundation Stage   51
6 Main judgements   58

Epilogue   81

Index   82

Foreword

No matter what responsibilities you carried as a deputy, or an assistant head, or a faculty leader, headship takes you into a whole new world. It comes home to you when you're suddenly aware that your short walk from the car park sends ripples all around the building – faces glimpsed at windows, someone dawdling through the entrance hall to be the first to say 'Good morning'. Then there's your chair, and the desk, and the awesome realisation that, in the end, everything that happens in this place is down to you.

It's not a feeling that ever goes away, either, because the role of headship changes all the time. The wise head knows that years of service aren't necessarily enough when it comes to keeping ahead of the game. Brand new challenges will appear all the time, right up to and into your final year in the job.

Help is at hand, of course, from fellow heads, advisers, parents, colleagues, the youngsters themselves. Importantly, though, there'll be times when you just want to read quietly and reflect upon the thoughts and ideas of others who've trodden the same road. That's where this series comes in. What you'll find in these short and focussed books is, simply, 'words from the wise' – advice from people who know that your time is precious and are ready to link arms with you and take you, metaphorically, to one side and say,

'Look, this is something I know quite a bit about. Let me run you through a few things that work pretty well. Then, my friend, it's up to you.'

There's no doubt that for even the most confident schools, the prospect of an inspection visit from an Ofsted team is daunting. For the leadership team and governors there's the worry that the inspection team will discover something obvious that's been missed, or that their focus of attention won't be on cherished values and achievements.

As time has gone on, however, and schools have been inspected twice or more, those on both sides of the process have grown to understand each other rather more. Schools – the majority of effective ones anyway – have accordingly felt generally easier about it all.

But then, in September 2005, came a new inspection framework – one that, in Bill Laar's words in his introduction to this book,

"… is not merely a refinement of previous practice but a radical departure from it."

So what do schools face now? A return to a climate of anxiety?

Bill's answer – reassuringly from someone of such vast experience of each layer of the inspection process – is that schools can be at least as confident about Ofsted's visits as they ever were, and that if they've properly prepared themselves, the framework offers them every opportunity to show their strengths and achievements.

The key to inspection now, Bill reminds us, is self-evaluation, a process recorded on the all-important Self-Evaluation Form (SEF)

For me, Bill's advice here on the whole process of self-evaluation, and on completion of the SEF itself, is masterly – an object lesson in how to provide practical, intelligible and concise guidance in an area where misunderstanding and confusion are always possible. Always, he points out, the SEF should be accurate, clear and jargon-free. It should avoid unsubstantiated assertions, and back up everything with what Bill calls, "reasonable evidence of realisation, implementation or achievement."

The combined process of self-evaluation and inspection should enhance rather than distract from the understanding that everything we do in school is focussed on the learning and well being of the children in our care. We've always known that. Now, though, the principle's underlined for us by the government's "Every Child Matters" Framework, and in a chapter with that title, Bill Laar reminds us that a good Ofsted team will now measure everything against the ECM agenda. He goes on to explain exactly what this means and what a good school will be doing to meet the criteria.

Importantly, Bill believes that the current framework isn't the end –

that the principle of self-evaluation will move on, which is why, throughout, he emphasises the need for schools to turn to fellow professionals who can be critical friends.

For me, this is the book no head, or aspirant head, or governor, can be without. Every school, after all, is going to be inspected, and every school surely needs some advice and support. That said, Bill Laar – experienced, down to earth, deeply committed to schools and the children we teach – is the right person to provide it.

Gerald Haigh

Introduction

The new inspection process, in operation since September 2005, is not merely a refinement of previous practice but a radical departure from it. Many teachers believe that the changes suggest a cursory, and possibly combative, form of inspection that will make it difficult for schools to present themselves in the best light. They are uncertain as to why the focus on teaching is significantly reduced. They are concerned about the strong emphasis on performance measures. They wonder whether this and the complex matter of contextual value added will determine the inspection outcome. This unease is also felt in other quarters:

> Such performance measures are vital, but inspection reports should also convey the character of a school. (*TES*)

The Chief Inspector has responded reassuringly to calm fears. He accepts that the new inspection system 'raises the bar' but points out:

> We cannot seriously argue that the levels of achievement considered acceptable in schools ten years ago will be acceptable today . . . there is more, much more to do if *all* of our pupils are to achieve well and become good and productive citizens. Hence the need to ensure that our accountability arrangements are fit for purpose as we head into the latter part of the first decade of the 21st century.

He sees the following as the benefits of the new inspection system:

- Smaller inspection teams and fewer inspection days will leave schools less exhausted by the process and enable them to move on more quickly with the vital task of raising standards.

- The new approach will promote dialogue between the school and the inspectors and make more appropriate demands on all those working in schools.

- The inspection system begins with the premise that the school is best placed to recognise its own strengths and weaknesses and should be capable of planning actions which will sort out the weaknesses and improve the strengths. The school that knows itself well is better placed to make improvements in the future.

- The move to greater self-evaluation puts the onus on the school to demonstrate to inspectors how well they think they are progressing. They will need to provide robust evidence, collected by themselves, and show they can diagnose where their school improvement priorities need to be focused.

- Where a school can demonstrate secure systems for school improvement, then the new inspection process will support the school's work in a positive way.

- The new style of inspection will place particular emphasis on the value added by schools to their pupils' attainment and general education. The new form of school Performance and Assessment Report (PANDA), showing information based on 'contextual value added' will challenge schools to substantiate the evaluations they make of their performance and to justify ambitious claims.

- *With more frequent inspections, every three years, parents will have a more regular external perspective on how their child's school is progressing.*

(Abstracted from the Chief Inspector's address to the DfES/Ofsted Governors' Conference, 29th September 2005)

Let me express a personal viewpoint, subjective but based on years of experience of schools. It seems to me that in many respects this is a golden age of primary education:

- Ofsted has formally declared that teaching has never been better (and, by implication, that learning is equally effective).

- Pupils have made extraordinary progress in literacy and numeracy according to standardised data.

- The leadership and management of schools are refined, developed and sophisticated to a degree that would have been unrecognisable even to accomplished heads a decade ago.

- Teachers have an unprecedented understanding of the purpose of formative assessment and how to apply the information it supplies.

- Schools' provision for English as an Additional Language (EAL) learners is increasingly effective.

- The resourcing and teaching of Information and Communication Technology (ICT) have never been better.

I could go on, but I believe these are just some of the reasons why schools can feel confident about the case they bring to inspection, whatever form it takes, and be happy to accept recommendations for developments that will further enhance their performance.

This book is designed to help schools respond effectively to inspection and to present themselves in ways that will do justice to their work, to their achievement, attainment and progress and to the value they add to their pupils' education.

Bill Laar

Chapter 1

The framework for inspecting schools

It's all change in the inspection process (re-invented more often, it seems, than an ageing rock star!). The current schedule is very different – from now on: *the school is the inspector.*

This chapter covers the new process, including:

■ the rationale underlying new inspections

■ the inspection format and how it is applied

■ schools' vital contribution to the process and the role of self-evaluation.

The inspection process will deliver a judgement on the overall effectiveness and efficiency of the school by inspecting and evaluating:

■ achievements and standards, including pupils' personal development and well-being

■ the quality of provision, including the quality of teaching and learning

■ leadership and management

■ where it is relevant, standards and quality of the Foundation Stage.

There will be an additional important judgement about:

- the capacity of the school to make improvement
- the school's ability to accurately assess the quality of its own provision.

There is nothing new or unfamiliar here, of course.

However, the new inspection form is radically different from previous inspection practice. And it isn't just a matter of a large reduction in inspection days or subjects not being inspected or some teachers not being observed at all.

To make the best of the new system and to work effectively with it, we have to understand that:

> The great difference lies in a *changed perception* of how inspection can bring about school improvement most effectively. The procedural changes (e.g. less time spent in lesson observation, a huge reduction in the documentation required of schools), all flow from that 'new philosophy' of school inspection.

What is the critical difference in the new inspection format?

It is this: it puts the onus on schools to be their own inspectors. It is a major step in the self-regulation of schools. It implies that schools themselves are able and competent to be the best judges of their own performance, in partnership with detached external evaluators. This radical change in the process, which seeks to make inspection a truly collaborative exercise, with inspectors really 'doing it *with* schools' rather than '*to* them', is possible for a number of reasons:

- the existence of comprehensive and more reliable data about school performance
- the growing ability to make authoritative judgements about the value added by schools to pupils' educational achievement

■ the increasingly sophisticated, exhaustive and rigorous self-evaluation processes undertaken and constantly maintained by schools.

Inspectors are now equipped to make informed judgements based on extensive school self-evaluation and powerful data, rather than inspired guesses sometimes fuelled by personal prejudices and 'baggage'. Their job is to evaluate, using all the information they possess, whether the school's picture of itself is accurate and to identify what improvements the school needs to make. If schools perceive themselves as good, how do they substantiate the claim?

■ Timetable for the inspection

Both the head teacher and the governing body will receive a phone call between two and five days before an inspection is to take place. Once the school has been informed that inspection is imminent, the head teacher will ensure that she/he or a nominated senior member of staff will be available within the next day or so to receive the follow-up call from the lead inspector.

The phone call
Prepare in advance:
　　When you get the phone call what will you do?
　　When will you meet with staff?
　　What will happen if the head teacher is absent when the call comes through?
　　What will the secretary do if the call comes to her/him?

As soon as possible after this initial call to establish the timing of the inspection, the lead inspector will contact the head teacher to discuss arrangements. This contact will take the form of a substantial telephone call in which the lead inspector will complete the following business:

■ Establish when the School Evaluation Form (SEF) was last updated: whether there have been any major changes since then.

■ Describe what the inspection will be like and provide any clarification the head teacher requires.

■ Explain that feedback will be provided for any staff whose teaching is observed. When informing staff of this, it will be stressed that judgements about the quality of teaching in the school will be based not merely on the sample of lesson observations but on other evidence such as pupil attainment and progress, 'Every child matters' outcomes, and pupil response.

■ Raise the possibility of joint lesson observations, involving the head teacher or nominated senior member of staff and member of inspection team. This is an optional activity. Schools are free to decline the offer. However, it is patently sensible and desirable to seize the opportunity of shared observations, which would enable the head/senior staff to be explicit about their perceptions of good teaching and the ways in which they promote it through the school.

Heads are free to decide which teachers are to be nominated for observation and may usefully give the reasons for their selection:

– 'This teacher in her first year is growing perceptibly in confidence and performance . . . '

– 'This teacher is working successfully with a challenging Yr 4 class containing a high proportion of pupils with pronounced special needs . . . '

– 'I intend to put this teacher forward as a lead teacher for Literacy.'

The inspector engaged in the observation will require the head to make the formal evaluation of the lesson and will not share her/his personal judgements. In effect, the inspector is not merely evaluating the quality of the teaching but the head's evaluation of it. (In this context, heads may find the criteria for effective teaching in Chapter 6 helpful.)

- Point out the need to talk to individual members of staff outside lessons and make initial arrangements for this.

- Check that all the necessary documentation will be available.

- Discuss the possibilities of a brief pre-inspection meeting, to discuss purely administrative matters.

- Ask the head teacher to invite the Chair of Governors or a representative to a brief meeting during inspection, and to hear oral feedback at the close of inspection.

- Establish that oral feedback will occur on the last day after the end of the inspection. The inspection team will describe and explain their conclusions, why judgements have been made and what the school needs to do to improve, to the head teacher and senior staff and, if possible, to the Chair of Governors. The written report, available within three weeks, will contain no surprising or unexpected information.

- Establish that the school has advised parents/carers of the inspection using the standard letter and whether responses to the accompanying questionnaire have been received. These should be made available to the lead inspector on the first day.

This telephone meeting will result in the identification and confirmation of main issues, line of enquiry and 'trails' that will be followed in the course of the inspection. The process, however, will be flexible; during the course of the inspection some hypotheses may well be confirmed early on to the satisfaction of inspectors, and require no further pursuit or investigation; in some cases, other suppositions may prove less well founded, or new issues may arise and matters be called to the attention of inspectors that call for further scrutiny.

Do not underestimate the importance of this second 'business' phone call (as opposed to the earlier one to notify the school of the timetable for inspection). Put aside an hour for this. Have a pad available to make notes and a copy of your SEF for reference. Be alert. Listen carefully to what is said, for example, about proposed trails, about the shape of inspection on the first day, and of conclusions the team may seem to have drawn from your SEF. Try to achieve the following by the end of the conversation:

■ Ensure that you have arrived with the inspector at a shared understanding about school attainment, standards and trends.

■ Obtain from the inspector an indication of two/three or more points in the SEF that have created a positive impression on her/him.

■ Clarify any points of significance in the SEF content that are obscure, unclear or perplexing to the inspector.

The self-evaluation process

At the heart of the inspection will be the school's self-evaluation process, summarised in the School Evaluation Form. The self-evaluation process shapes a school's drive for improvement and drives its inspection.

The school will provide the inspection team, immediately before the inspection, with a copy of the SEF. This will, in effect, tell the 'story' of the school, its pupils, their education and performance. The SEF will be 'pre-populated' with specific data, much of it externally provided. In addition to the SEF, inspectors will have:

■ the school's Performance and Assessment Report (PANDA), and

■ the school's previous inspection report.

These three documents will be used to prepare a pre-inspection briefing (PIB) for the inspection team. This briefing will be made available to the school on the first morning of the inspection.

The PIB will flag up the main lines of enquiry and debate, the inspection 'trails' or lines of investigation proposed for the school, at least at the outset of the inspection. These 'trails' or lines of enquiry may be modified and changed by initial findings; when, for example, a team is satisfied that it has sufficient evidence to preclude the need for further search.

> The PIB, in an important sense, represents Ofsted's intention that there should be no mystery or hidden agenda, no element of a guessing game, no subterfuge or bluff and counter-bluff about the process.

The PIB sets out what the inspection wants to confirm about the school's own evaluation and the accuracy of its judgements, and to clarify what may be unclear. The team will seek to form a true picture from all the information and data presented to it in the limited time available.

The inspection team's duties

The inspection team will require from the school:

■ the current development/improvement/management plan

■ the timetable for the days in school by staff, including the extracurricular timetable

■ information about interruptions to normal routine during inspection activities.

The latter reinforces the concept of an inspection process that seeks to view the school as it is. The inspection must fit around the school's timetable, routines and planned activities, and not the reverse, with the school having to re-invent itself for the purpose of being inspected. As a consequence, inspections are often conducted against a backdrop of classes absent on educational outings, or staff elsewhere on particular professional business, e.g. INSET (in-service training). In other words, inspectors see things in the context of the everyday life of a school.

Underlying the approach is the fact that the team will be able to test its hypotheses about the school not merely through active scrutiny of what is happening, but against a formidable battery of evidence and data.

Inspectors may need to see the following documents during the course of the inspection:

- school analysis of performance data – including use of any value-added evaluation system and analysis of ethnicity group performance

- data on attainment on entry

- governing body minutes

- financial information showing the whole-school picture if this is not already present in the SEF

- curriculum organisation

- records of external monitoring by bodies or individuals (e.g. the local authority)

- school brochures

- specific school policies, e.g. on health and safety; teaching and learning; inclusion and child protection

- any significant up-to-date contextual information, e.g. bids for specific funding or status; reorganisation proposals; major building developments.

In addition to these documents or information, the school may wish to bring other information to the attention of the inspection team.

The school will also need to have the following documentation available in their normal school location:

- records of classroom monitoring, and action subsequently taken

- records relating to vulnerable children

- special educational needs (SEN) files/Individual Education Plans (IEPs).

Schemes of work and any subject policies may be consulted by the team in the course of the inspection in classroom locations. It is likely that documents will be consulted only as the need arises.

Pupils' workbooks and all evidence of their work and learning will continue to provide crucial evidence in relation to the inspection. The scrutiny of such work, however, will not be as intensive as in the former inspection process.

This change is due not merely to the greatly reduced time available but to the belief that vital and secure evidence about levels of attainment and pupil progress is available from other sources. However, inspectors may take a more prolonged view of pupils' work if they have reason to feel that a particular subject or the attainment and progress of a group of pupils requires it.

Samples of pupils' work in the core subjects, arranged around three levels of ability, will continue to be required for scrutiny.

Inspectors are required to be flexible and responsive to emerging issues

Inspectors will spend much of the inspection on site gathering evidence by:

- first-hand observation

- talking to staff, pupils and others in the school

- tracking school processes such as evaluation and performance management

- interviewing members of staff: head teacher and senior management team and almost certainly core curriculum leaders, the Special Educational Needs Coordinator (SENCO) and the Early Years Coordinator

- analysing samples of current and recent work

- joining meetings, such as school council or management meetings, and directly observing management processes such as the monitoring of teaching

- analysing records relating to pupils with special educational needs, including individual education plans, statements

- tracking case studies of vulnerable pupils such as those with learning difficulties, and disabilities, and children in care.

Inspectors will gather and analyse their findings on evidence forms.

Evidence forms

The evidence form (EF) is the document for recording all first-hand evidence.

All EFs will contain a statement of the main focus of the evidence-gathering activity, relating to one or more of the inspection issues.

In the case of lesson observations, the context will give a brief descriptive account of what the lesson is about, its objectives and its outcomes.

The evaluation section of the EF provides brief evaluative comment. Descriptive detail will be sparingly employed and then only to illustrate points. In the evaluation of teaching, a connection must be made to the impact it has on learners' progress and personal development.

All EFs must contain a summary. In the case of lessons, this will clearly identify clearly the main strengths and weaknesses that can be fed back to teachers.

The observation of teaching

Inspectors will not always observe completed lessons; in many cases inspectors will not be present in lessons for longer then 20 or 30 minutes, and sometimes less.

In larger schools not all teachers will be observed teaching.

Foundation subjects will not be inspected, as such, though evidence and evaluations presented by the school, and evidence acquired by inspectors in relation to them, are likely to contribute to final inspection judgements.

The overall judgement of teaching, based on a four-point scale, will depend mainly on the quality of teaching as demonstrated by the outcomes for the learners in terms of their progress and personal development, including their attitudes and behaviour, and the safeguarding of their health and safety. (This critically important matter will be explored further in the section on Teaching and Learning).

Ofsted guidance on the use of Evidence Forms stresses that the accurate completion of the summary is a most important contribution to the overall view of the school and what it needs to do to improve.

A common grading scale will be used in making inspection judgements:

– Grade 1 Outstanding
– Grade 2 Good
– Grade 3 Satisfactory
– Grade 4 Inadequate.

At the end of the inspection, the team must decide which grade the school falls into.

Provision causing concern

If inspectors judge that a school's overall effectiveness is inadequate, it will fall into one of two categories: Special measures or Notice to improve. The distinction between the two is as follows:

■ Special measures: Schools which require special measures because they are failing to give learners an acceptable standard of education, and where the persons responsible for leading, managing or governing the school are not demonstrating the capacity to secure the necessary improvement.

■ Notice to improve: Schools which require significant improvement because they are performing significantly less well than they might reasonably be expected to perform. A school which is currently failing to provide an acceptable standard of education, but has the capacity to improve, will also be in this category.

When a draft report includes either of these judgements, the governing body must be given five days notice to comment on the draft before the report is finalised. Ofsted stresses that this action is rare 'since most schools emerge with credit from their inspections'.

To summarise, inspectors will be evaluating:

- how effectively performance is monitored and improved through quality assurance measures and self-assessment

- how effectively leaders and managers at all levels clearly direct improvement and promote the well-being of learners through high quality care, education and training

- how well equality of opportunity is promoted and discrimination tackled so that all learners achieve their potential

- the adequacy and suitability of staff, including the effectiveness of processes for recruitment and selection of staff, to ensure that learners are well taught and protected

- the adequacy and suitability of specialist equipment, learning resources and accommodation

- how effectively and efficiently resources are developed to achieve value for money.

Chapter 2
Self-evaluation

Given the emphasis on the institutions providing the essential evidence, the new inspection process requires a solid and authoritative self-evaluation by schools, enabling them to confidently point inspectors towards their findings. This chapter covers the following:

■ the purpose of self-evaluation

■ questions that help make self-evaluation effective

■ the construction of the SEF

■ the questions the SEF seeks to answer

■ the presentation of a SEF.

The key questions for self-evaluation are:

■ How well are we doing?

■ How do we know?

■ How can we do better?

Rigorous self-evaluation provides the most effective way of identifying strengths and weaknesses. When you know these, you can make your priorities for improvement.

Schools must use the evidence provided by self-evaluation to:

■ identify strengths and weaknesses and the implications for change

■ identify the key priorities

■ plan the action needed to bring about improvement.

The DfES has put in place what it describes as the New Relationship with Schools (NRWS). One of the principles of NRWS is that schools should have a single integrated development plan.

The development plan will contain elements of previous plans that continue to have an impact on the work of the school.

The plan will be based on a rigorous assessment of what the school needs to do.

It will set out the strengths and weaknesses of the school.

It will state priorities for dealing with the weaknesses and other necessary areas of development.

The plan of action will be precisely defined. Resources will be costed and linked to improvement activities. Timescales for action will be established. Provision for review and assessment of the impact the action is having will be built in. Monitoring responsibilities will be allocated. It is essential that schools maintain throughout the annual review cycle a regular check on whether the improvement plan and activities are having the required impact. This review may lead to modification of targets and activities and to a refocusing of resources. It is likely to affect in some ways the nature of the next development plan.

What should schools evaluate?

Evaluation is a gradual or partial process in the sense that not everything can, or needs to be, reviewed at one and the same time. At the very top of school's priorities is the need to know with certainty how well pupils are performing in terms of:

■ their overall standards of attainment

■ the standards attained by different groups within the school, including girls and boys, children with special educational needs, the gifted and the talented, and learners from different minority ethnic groups

■ the progress learners make over periods of time: between entering school and the end of the Foundation Stage, between the Foundation Stage and the end of Key Stage 1, between Key Stage 1 and 2, and indeed over shorter intervals of time: over and within yearly periods

■ the outcomes from the provision for learners' personal development and well-being. This will include especially how far personal development and well-being match the five outcomes advocated by the Every Child Matters agenda. The ECM agenda and its implications for inspection are considered in detail in Chapter 3.

Schools will also need to assess the quality, and impact on standards of attainment and achievement, of the following areas and aspects:

■ provision; this includes teaching, the curriculum, and the care, guidance and support provided for learners

■ leadership and management at all levels, including the governance of the school

■ features and objectives specific to the school

■ links between the school and other services and providers.

Thus, staff and governors of schools will need to evaluate consistently:

■ the impact and effectiveness of their strategies for improvement

■ the impact of improvement strategies and actions on the learning, attainment, achievement and welfare of the pupils

■ the effectiveness of the resources employed.

How should schools evaluate the quality of their provision?

Schools are free to use the process/model that provides them with the clearest picture of the effectiveness of their improvement strategies. School Improvement Partners (SIPs), local authority advisers and other accredited consultants can offer valuable support to schools in carrying out their review, posing challenging questions, making constructive criticism of the school's perceptions and evaluations, and identifying other sources of evidence. They can act as critical readers of the School Evaluation Form. Primary head teachers may well find that this role of informed, detached critical friend can be very effectively and inexpensively performed by fellow head teachers on a *quid pro quo* basis. Such evaluation arrangements can also enhance the professional insight and awareness of participants/'partners'.

Does our self-evaluation lead to action to achieve the school's longer-term goals for development?

In drawing up a development plan, schools need to distinguish between the short-term annual and operational priorities (e.g. a focus over a year on a few key areas and a limited number of tasks) and the longer-term strategic objectives.

In response either to a full-scale evaluation or assessment of an aspect of the school's work, a development plan should do the following:

- identify a limited number of main priorities for improvement in relation to benefits for learners

- focus on the continual improvement of outcomes for learners, their academic standards and personal development

- include specific responsibilities, timescales, interim review dates, measurable success criteria and targets linked to learners' attainment and progress

- identify and be able to justify the cost benefits in terms of learners' outcomes.

The School Evaluation Form

The SEF is not, in itself, self-evaluation. It is the place where a summary of the findings of a thorough self-evaluation is recorded.

How Ofsted inspectors use the SEF

Inspectors use the SEF, the summary of the school's self-evaluation, together with the previous inspection report and the PANDA report (see Chapter 6, where the role of the PANDA in the inspection is fully explored), for the following purposes:

- as a starting point for discussion with the school

- to decide what to focus on when planning the inspection

- to identify inconsistencies between the SEF and the pre-inspection evidence gathered from sources such as the PANDA

- to evaluate the quality of leadership and management from evidence contained within the SEF

- to investigate important issues that the SEF appears to have glossed over or misrepresented

- to identify important features of the school work that will be part of the inspection process.

The SEF will be used and referred to throughout the inspection.

The inspection will seek to establish how well the senior staff and the governors know the strengths of the school and the areas and aspects that require improvement.

In this respect, it is important that schools are explicit about areas of weakness. If schools fail to bring these to light, then inspectors, who will most certainly find them, may draw negative conclusions about the effectiveness of monitoring and even about the quality of leadership and management.

In pursuing this, inspectors will examine the claims made by the SEF and then require schools to demonstrate the evidence that substantiates them.

Completing the SEF

The SEF needs to be clearly and simply written. Jargon and obscure or ambiguous language should be avoided.

The SEF must be accurate and clear. The information it provides must be honest and be clearly presented.

The SEF should be updated to be in line with the normal cycles of school improvement. If this is done regularly, it should not be a time-consuming bureaucratic process.

The SEF questions should be answered by making clear judgements.

Each answer should be substantiated/justified with a brief summary of the evidence.

Assertion (i.e. a claim that is not, nor can be, substantiated by evidence) should be avoided since it will not be treated as valid evidence by inspectors.

Schools should seek, as far as possible, to back claims and statements with reasonable evidence of realisation, implementation or achievement. In effect: 'We're not just saying we did it; we're demonstrating how we know that specific action was productive in terms of pupil attainment, learning and progress.' It is important to understand that inspectors are likely to disregard what they perceive to be unsupported assertion.

So, for example, where data is available that allows for reference to test and examination results or attendance figures, this should be accompanied by:

- what the data told you

- what the school did as a result of this

- what the impact was on the learners' attainment, progress or well-being as a result of the action you took

- how you know this

- how you can be sure of this.

Refer to other reliable evidence where this is relevant, but use it selectively to support judgements. Schools can indicate in the SEF where more detailed evidence can be found, e.g. in subject files; classroom observations; pupils' work.

The summary of the evaluation of the five ECM ('Every Child Matters') outcomes should not merely comment on what the school has done to promote the outcomes but should describe the impact of the outcomes on the learners, i.e. how far pupils' progress, attainment and behaviour have been positively affected.

Reaching judgements in the SEF

At the end of each section of the SEF, schools are invited to make a summary judgement and grade. The grade will be made in line with the common grading scale used by Ofsted (see Chapter 1).

The overall summary judgement and grade must be composite. For example, in the achievement and standards section, the judgement must incorporate both the standards attained by learners and their progress over time. In this context, the critical element is the progress the learners make, even more than the standards achieved. This will be a significant matter for schools that struggle to raise pupils' attainment in adverse and economically disadvantaged circumstances.

In the Overall Effectiveness section, the composite judgement is a summary of all the other main judgements. In making this judgement, school leaders need to consider: the close link between learners' progress, the quality of provision and the effectiveness of leadership and management.

Leadership and management, including the effectiveness of governance, are judged primarily in terms of outcomes for learners.

Judgements about leadership and management will no longer be influenced by matters of style and charisma on the part of head teachers, on their capacity to present a plausible argument and to state a case in a persuasive and winning style. Instead, inspectors will look for well-substantiated evidence that pupils' attainment and progress are as good as they can be.

Failure on the part of a Governing Body to exercise satisfactorily their prescribed responsibility for the performance of a school, in providing for the attainment and well-being of pupils, would almost certainly lead to a critical evaluation of leadership and management overall.

Inspectors need to be convinced that Governors are playing an active hands-on role in the annual cycle of review, are conversant with the implications of the SEF and are themselves in a position to evaluate how effectively their school is providing for pupils' attainment, progress and well-being.

Structure of the SEF

Introduction to the school

Schools are invited to set out the key contextual factors to consider. Do this by responding to five questions on:

- special features of the school
- main features of the learners
- contextual and other factors that affect or influence school and pupil performance
- the main objectives of the school improvement/performance plan
- particular issues that the school would like to bring to the attention of the inspectors and other readers.

Schools may find it helpful to consider whether the following examples of 'special features' proposed in some SEFs have a particular resonance for them.

Significantly above-average results at end of Key Stage 2 in current year in comparison with similar schools and above average when compared with national results. This marks a notable and consistent upward trend over the past three years.

A strong emphasis on the fostering of the principles and practice underlying 'Excellence and Enjoyment' without losing the upward momentum in standards and attainment as reflected in SATs results.

Extensive provision for the creative and expressive arts. Important input by skilled external specialists, especially in dance, music, gymnastics and arts and design, allowing in a proportion of cases for the release of teachers for monitoring and planning purposes and small group teaching.

Significantly enlarged library provision, especially in terms of reference and non-fiction materials, the use of interactive whiteboards in every classroom and good ICT provision, over the past year, have enhanced children's learning and contributed to raised standards of attainment.

School-based INSET is emphasising and helping teachers to understand the link between the effectiveness of their teaching and children's attainment and enhanced achievement.

The tracking system adopted and developed by the school monitors attainment on an individual, class and whole-year group basis and sets relevant, soundly based targets for individual pupil progress.

Setting in English and Maths from Yrs 3-6 has provided focused teaching in order to challenge higher achieving pupils and consolidate learning for pupils with SEN. Setting is making an appreciable contribution to raising attainment, especially in Maths performance.

The views of learners, parents and other stakeholders

This section provides an opportunity for a brief account of the way in which the school gathers and acts upon the views of its main stakeholders. The school is invited to review its evidence in response to three questions:

- How does the school gather its views and how often?

- What are the views?

- What action has the school taken in response to the views?

Schools canvass and collect the views of stakeholders in various ways, through:

- school and class councils

- questionnaires to parents and pupils

- 'focus groups' involving parents/carers and a broad range of members of the community

- interviews with parents, including home visits, on entry of children to school

- workshops and seminars

- formal occasions such as school concerts, music presentations, display of pupils' work, open evenings.

Statements of the following kind, canvassed in a range of schools are exemplars of information that has been illuminating, has endorsed particular measures and, in some cases, has led to the implementation of specific action.

> *Children attending school for the first time are immediately made to feel welcome and secure. They look forward to coming in each day. The parents also find a welcoming atmosphere. Their views and worries are listened to.*
>
> (Views of a small group of 'first-time' parents)

> *This is a school that makes a supply teacher feel part of the team and not simply someone pulled in off the street to fill a gap and as soon forgotten. It is an attitude that helps you to teach at your best.*
>
> (An experienced supply teacher)

> *Our opinions and views are listened to and respected. We feel we are making a real contribution to the children's education and that we are needed. The school is helping us to develop professionally.*
>
> (A learning assistant)

> *Breakfast Club is a very good idea. We like the chance to talk with our friends because it is quiet. We think it would be a good idea if*

*we could have music during the breakfast, especially if we could pick
the music ourselves.*

> (Children commenting on recently established breakfast club)

*The Parents' and Children's Noticeboard is very helpful and
interesting. We like the chance to contribute to it.*

> (Foundation Stage parent)

*We were impressed by the way in which the children generally
responded with confidence and enthusiasm and participated in a
very positive way.*

> (Visiting theatre group)

*Parents, especially of younger children, have suggested that they
would like an opportunity to meet once a term in class groups, that is
with other parents in their child's class. This would give them a
chance to discuss matters and share ideas that relate more
immediately to their own child. They want to stress that they remain
interested in whole school matters.*

> (Parent Governor)

*Children in Yrs 5 and 6 would like the chance to cycle to school.
Could the school organise this and make space for bicycles?*

> (School Council)

*The Governors are delighted to acknowledge the big progress that has
been made in English as reflected in the SATs at Key Stages 1 and 2.
We realise that progress is also being made in Mathematics but we
are puzzled by the very large gap in attainment between English and
Maths. We would have expected that progress could have been made
more easily in Maths.*

> (Governing Body)

Achievements and standards

Many schools will regard this as perhaps the most significant section of
all and, in some respects, the most challenging in terms of accurate and
informative response.

Achievement

This is the measure of learners' knowledge, understanding and skills in relation to their capabilities. It reflects the progress they have made and whether they are working to their capacity. What is crucial here is the value that a school adds to pupil performance and whether learners are doing as well as they can (see the *Achievement and standards* section in Chapter 6 for a full discussion of this).

Standards

By this is meant the level of knowledge, understanding and skill that learners reach compared with learners of the same age nationally, according to National Curriculum levels and Early Learning Goals.

To provide a reliable picture of standards, judgements need to be focused on the last academic year for which reliable data is available and on trends over time, perhaps three to four years.

Ensure data is accurate, and gives a fair and just view of the school. Express any reservations and present supporting evidence.

Judgements are also required on the standards and progress reached by different groups of learners in school: girls and boys: learners from ethnic groups; pupils with English as an additional or second language; pupils who may lead a mobile lifestyle. The judgements will need to be accompanied by explanation.

In addition to judgements on overall school performance, it is essential to include brief judgements on standards in foundation subjects.

Learners' personal development and well-being

This section requires evidence of what the school has done to improve learners' personal development. The main evidence that schools may offer apart from the data on attendance, exclusions and punctuality will be found in the measures that schools take to provide for the Every Child Matters outcomes (see Chapter 3). However, schools must remember that it is the learners' development and the extent to which they are meeting the outcomes that are of primary importance. (See the *Personal development and well-being* section of Chapter 6 for examples of good provision.)

The quality of provision

This incorporates three important elements:

■ the quality of teaching

■ curriculum provision

■ guidance and support of learners.

Central to this section will be the quality of teaching. Only some lessons will be observed, and often just part of the lesson. Provision is measured in terms of pupil progress. It must be substantiated by hard evidence.

Curriculum

Schools will need to make well-substantiated judgements on the curriculum and the care, guidance and support they offer. If aspects and elements of either the curriculum or of care provision are not statutorily compliant, then this must be made clear, together with reasons for the shortcoming.

When deciding how the curriculum and other activities meet the range of needs and interests of learners, you need to look at:

■ the extent to which the curriculum or activities match learners' needs, aspirations and capabilities, building on prior attainment and experience

■ how far the curriculum meets external requirements and is responsive to local circumstances. Examples of this might include the following:
 – the need to modify the curriculum to ensure a sensitive, supportive and creative response to significant social change in a neighbourhood and school brought about by rapid demographic change
 – curriculum experience and orientation that enlarge children's awareness and understanding of social environments, circumstances and contexts radically different from their own
 – a curriculum that promotes understanding of and positive attitudes to racial issues
 – curriculum provision that clarifies and defines for children a local culture or social and industrial history arising from

particular local circumstances and establishes a sense of heritage and a pride in it

 – a curriculum emphasising and exploring significant elements deriving from particular locations or geographical features, e.g. proximity to the Continent; location in an important seaport

■ the extent to which the provision enables and encourages learners to be healthy and stay safe

■ the extent to which learners have opportunities to develop enterprise, financial skills and the capacity to work in teams

■ the extent to which activities and, where appropriate, extended services contribute to learners' enjoyment and achievement (See Chapter 3 on the ECM agenda).

Finally, in this section on the quality of provision, the issues raised by the SEF about the guidance and support of learners are as follows:

■ the care, including integrated day care, advice, guidance and other support provided to learners to safeguard welfare, promote personal development and make good progress in their work

■ the quality and accessibility of advice, guidance and support for learners

■ the extent to which the school and any additional services contribute to the learners' capacity to be healthy, including vulnerable groups, such as looked-after children (see Chapter 3 on the ECM agenda. The issue of provision is fully discussed in Chapter 6).

The quality of leadership and management

The first point to make is that leadership and management are different entities and evaluation must take account of that. Head teachers as individuals may not be equally gifted in both areas. It is here that the point and importance of leadership teams or senior management teams are evident. The efficient deputy can, for example, provide practical input alongside an inspirational head. The head and deputy can rely on dynamism and enthusiasm from subject leaders.

This area of the SEF calls for rigorous, hard-edged judgements backed by authoritative evidence. This would include answers to the following questions:

- What monitoring is done? How does it identify problems and causes for concern? How are these dealt with?

- How is under-achievement identified and tackled? How is pupil progress tracked and analysed? What is done about the outcomes? How do senior managers and governors monitor value for money in relation to resources and staffing? How are governors effectively involved in the governance and leadership of the school? (Leadership and management are fully discussed in Chapter 6.)

Overall effectiveness and efficiency

In the final section of the SEF, all the previous evaluations are brought together. This section deals with three main questions:

- the overall effectiveness of the provision, including any extended services and its main strengths and weaknesses

- the effectiveness of any steps taken to promote improvements since the last inspection

- the school's capacity to make further improvements. Judgements and supportive evidence must reflect the judgements given elsewhere throughout the SEF.

Schools need to be rigorous in evaluation and totally honest in claims about the extent to which the school has improved since the previous inspection and what needs to be done to improve further.

The school must make rigorous evaluation of the ability of the school to improve in the future. This is not a particularly easy thing to do well: it calls less for optimism and wishful thinking than for an informed and very careful weighing up of circumstances, of real facts and the resources likely to be available to support development and improvement.

Some suggestions for developing your SEF

1 Above all, let the 'vision' you and your staff hold for the school, expressed in the development plan in all its important detail, be the starting point and basis for the content of the SEF.

2 Use particular occasions such as the preparation of the termly head teacher's report to Governors, the various staff meetings for management and curriculum purposes, and even the innumerable informal professional encounters and exchanges that make up the life of a school to note, record, assemble and document data, commentary, material that could contribute valuably to the strands of evidence that make up the SEF.

3 Read a range of SEFs. They are obtainable on the Internet, from local authorities, from head teacher colleagues. Pay particular attention to SEFs provided by schools similar in type to yours. They will serve a variety of purposes:
   a   to reinforce confidence in the model you are constructing;
   b   to cause you to reflect on your content and especially on elements you may have considered insufficiently important to justify comment or elaboration.
   c   to alert you to issues that need more extended commentary;
   d   to provide in some cases presentations so close to your own patterns of action that statements can be helpfully and positively adapted.

4 Provide an opportunity for all staff to contribute to the building of the evidence base. A readily available, easy-to-complete proforma would enable teachers/learning assistants and all other staff to record personal observations of school practice, significant comments from visitors and sources external to the school, and issues or incidents that illuminate and explicate the life of the school.

■ Model SEF

You can find a 'model' SEF in the Resources section of the David Fulton website (www.fultonpublishers.co.uk). We are indebted to the head teacher, Mr Neil Baker, and the staff of Audley Primary School, Birmingham, for this SEF, presented by the school in one of the later 'trial' inspections. It is an exhaustive example, perhaps overly so, but does place emphasis on justifying its claims by reference to evidence.

Chapter 3
'Every Child Matters'

The current inspection framework checks a school against the priorities of the '*Every Child Matters*' framework, so a well-managed inspection will constantly connect with the new direction from the DfES.

This chapter covers the following:

- the 'Every Child Matters' (ECM) agenda, its purpose and its structure

- the link between the agenda and pupils' attainment, achievement and progress

- practical ways in which the outcomes can be provided for across the curriculum

- the link between the ECM agenda and inclusion

- providing for spiritual, moral, social and cultural development.

The 'Every Child Matters' agenda

The 'Every Child Matters' (ECM) agenda had its genesis in the green paper *Every Child Matters* and the Children Act of 2004. The government legislation, in response to disturbing high-profile cases of negligence and ill-treatment of young children, is designed to ensure that all concerned institutions, organisations and individuals are committed to coherent and comprehensive provision for the welfare and protection of the young, in all circumstances.

Of course, it hardly needs saying that schools, with very few exceptions, have always been devoted to the well-being of children, have been places where they were not merely cared for but cherished as well. But the 'Every Child Matters' agenda is something fresh. It sets out in formal, explicit detail the needs, proper expectations and rights of children and the actions and policies that organisations must adopt to ensure these are realised.

Schools, in meeting the needs of children, need no longer be dependent on instinct, right intentions, good precedent and admired practice. In summary, children have a right to the following:

- physical and mental health ('being healthy'): so that they enjoy good health and a healthy lifestyle

- protection from harm and neglect ('staying safe'): so their welfare is safeguarded and they know how to stay safe

- education and training ('enjoying and achieving'): so that they enjoy and make good progress in learning, leisure and personal development

- to be enabled to make a contribution to society ('making a positive contribution') so that they join in, take responsibility and play a productive part in the community

- achieving economic well-being: so that they have a good start in life and are able to achieve their full potential.

The ECM agenda incorporates all the important matters at the centre of inspection. Ofsted points out that since the well-being of children has always been a major concern of inspections, the need to engage with ECM outcomes is not new. But it is now more significant, no longer merely an important part of the inspection, but the main focus of the inspection itself. Every aspect of the evaluation schedule will be judged in relation to its effectiveness in providing for and promoting the outcomes of the ECM agenda.

The effectiveness of provision for the ECM agenda will be judged not primarily on the grounds of its ambition or expansiveness but on the impact it has on the outcomes and the extent to which it brings about their realisation.

What steps will inspectors take to judge the ECM outcomes? In their inspection of the main areas of the schedule, they will evaluate the quality of ECM outcomes. The sections below indicate how the ECM outcomes are incorporated within the main areas of the inspection schedule.

▨ Achievements and standards

Inspectors will evaluate:

- learners' success in achieving relevant and challenging targets, learning goals, accredited levels and qualifications

- trends in terms of success for individuals and groups over periods of time

- significant variations between groups of learners

- the degree to which the standard of pupils' work matches up to clear learning goals

- the progress made by pupils from previous levels of attainment and potential; significant variation in terms of progress from previous levels between particular groups of pupils.

In the context of achievements and standards, inspectors will also seek to evaluate:

- the degree to which pupils enjoy their work (All these areas of evaluation will provide evidence about the ECM outcome 'enjoying and achieving')

- the emotional development of learners (ECM outcomes 'being healthy' and 'staying safe')

- the extent to which pupils have regard to and undertake safe behaviour and follow a healthy lifestyle (ECM outcomes 'being healthy' and 'staying safe')

- pupils' spiritual, moral, social, and cultural development (ECM outcomes 'enjoying and achieving' and 'making a positive contribution')

- pupils' contribution to the community (ECM outcome 'making a positive contribution')

- the acquisition of skills relevant to the social and economic well-being of pupils (ECM outcomes 'staying safe' and 'making a positive contribution').

The quality of provision

How effective are teaching, training and learning?

Inspectors will evaluate:

- how well teaching and resources promote learning, meet all of pupils' needs and relevant course and programme requirements (ECM outcomes 'staying safe' and 'making a positive contribution')

- the effectiveness of assessment in planning, monitoring and identifying pupils' progress (ECM outcome 'enjoying and achieving')

- the identification of and provision for additional learning needs (ECM outcome 'enjoyment and achieving')

- the extent of parents'/carers' engagement in their children's learning and development (ECM outcome 'enjoying and achieving').

How well do programmes and activities meet the needs and interests of learners?

Inspectors will evaluate:

- the extent to which educational programmes and activities build on pupils' previous experience and attainment to meet their aspirations and match their potential (ECM outcomes 'enjoying and achieving' and 'achieving economic well-being')

- how far the whole curriculum satisfies external requirements and is in tune with local circumstances (ECM outcomes 'making a positive contribution' and 'achieving economic well-being')

■ How far pupils' enjoyment, attainment and achievement gain from enrichment programmes and activities and extended services (ECM outcomes 'enjoying and achieving'; 'making a positive contribution' and 'achieving economic well-being')

■ How far this extended provision enhances pupils' capacity to stay safe and healthy (ECM outcomes 'being healthy' and 'staying safe').

How well are learners guided and supported?

Inspectors will evaluate:

■ the nature and the quality of care, guidance and any support designed to promote personal development, secure welfare and contribute to the attainment of high standards (ECM outcomes 'being healthy,' 'staying safe' and 'enjoying and achieving')

■ the quality of guidance and advice to pupils to support their understanding of and learning in relation to particular programmes (ECM outcome 'enjoying and achieving').

How effective are leadership and management in raising achievement and supporting all learners?

Inspectors will evaluate:

■ the effectiveness of quality assurance and self-assessments in monitoring and improving performance

■ the effectiveness of managers at all levels in providing high-quality education, leadership, training and care directed to the improvement and well-being of pupils

■ how far learners are enabled to achieve their potential because of the assured provision of equality of opportunity and the absence of any forms of discrimination

■ the quality, effectiveness and adequacy of learning resources, specialised equipment and teaching and learning accommodation

- the provision, recruitment, and retention of good quality staff, able and sufficient to provide effectively for the teaching and care of learners

- the effective and efficient application of resources, learning materials and equipment to achieve value for money

- the quality and effectiveness of links with other providers, organisations and services, involved in education and extended provision, intended to promote learning and learners' well-being

- the effectiveness of governing bodies in discharging their obligations and responsibilities.

'Every Child Matters' good practice

The following sections run through the five ECM outcomes, highlighting what inspectors will look for, and the kind of judgements they make about them.

Examples are provided of steps that schools take to promote the outcomes. It may be helpful to ask yourself:

What similar statements could I make about my school?

How can I demonstrate our work and success in relation to these outcomes?

How well do learners adopt healthy lifestyles?

Inspectors are required to evaluate whether learners:

- take regular exercise including at least two hours of PE and sport a week

- know about and make healthy lifestyle choices

- where appropriate, understand the dangers of smoking and substance abuse – eat and drink healthily

- recognise signs of personal stress and develop strategies to manage it.

The following type of comment suggests a good inspection grade:

> Most learners have a good understanding of what is meant by a healthy lifestyle and what they should do to lead it. They demonstrate this in various practical ways. They engage in about two hours of organised PE, sport and games each week. Many of them take other opportunities, e.g. during playtimes and outside school, to take part in a range of physical activities.

> Learners have a good insight into what makes for healthy eating; they appreciate and enjoy the good quality well-balanced and ample school meals or bring, in the majority of cases, nutritious packed lunches. Many bring their own bottled water which they are able to drink when they need to or use the water fountains available in every classroom.

Examples of measures taken by schools

- New menus provided (to include halal/vegetarian options) as a result of concerns about quality and suitability raised in parent/pupil questionnaires.

- Water fountains have been set up around school; pupils encouraged to bring own water bottles and use them throughout the day.

- Diverse provision and equipment, including skipping ropes, a maze, short tennis areas, trampolines, dance bars and platforms and an imaginative play area, enable children to engage in a wide range of outside activities.

- The school has worked towards Active Mark, a national award for commitment to fitness and healthy lifestyles.

Education and training ('enjoying and achieving')

Inspectors are required to evaluate learners' attitudes, behaviour and attendance and other factors that indicate how well learners enjoy their education.

This kind of comment relates to an outstanding inspection grading:

Nearly all the learners demonstrate exemplary attitudes and impeccable behaviour. They achieve high levels of attendance and punctuality. They respond to staff with enthusiasm and pleasure and generally form happy and fulfilling relationships with other pupils. They are confident and secure and ready to take initiative.

They are deeply interested in their lessons, and readily become absorbed by their work, in which they take great pride. They consistently demonstrate expectations that what they are about to learn will be rewarding and exciting. They are eager to take part in whatever learning activities arise. They are proud of their school, and are ardent in expressing their affection and regard for it.

Measures taken by schools

- The school has invested in comprehensive provision of interactive whiteboard and high-quality software to enhance effective teaching and learning and to support work in the foundation subjects. All staff have been trained in the use of the material.

- School is building into lessons provision for the development of pupils' thinking skills and is providing opportunity for extracurricular philosophy sessions for older pupils.

- School is attempting to enhance pupils' learning through an enriched environment, educational visits to the wider community, practical science and environmental studies, through encounters with naturalists, visiting theatre and history presentation groups, and a wide range of art and music activities.

- School has made the raising of attainment and progress of pupils with SEN a main priority of its strategic plan. Special emphasis has been placed on the provision of a wide range of resources, including ICT materials to accelerate pupils' command of language and literacy.

- School makes family learning provision: IT, Literacy and Numeracy courses are offered each term in consultation with recipients.

Evaluating whether learners make a positive contribution to society

Inspectors should evaluate the extent to which learners:

- understand their rights and responsibilities

- show social responsibility and refrain from bullying and discrimination

- express their views at school with confidence that their voices will be heard

- initiate and manage a range of organised activities in school and community organisations.

This comment represents a good inspection grading:

Most learners develop a good sense of social responsibility. They understand the purpose of school rules and respond positively to them. In most age groups pupils have contributed to the framing of class rules.

Pupils generally demonstrate caring behaviour and concern for each other. They are active in resisting any suggestion of bullying or attempt at intimidation on anyone's part. They are confident about expressing their views and opinions and contributing to school decisions made through the medium of school and class councils. They listen sensibly to and take account of the views of others.

Measures taken by schools

- Pupils have produced a *Visitors' Guide to the School*, using photographic and communication technology to include illustrations and diagrams. They have devised a school quiz to accompany the guide book. They are currently planning a school trail.

- The active School Council enables pupils to make a valuable contribution to decision-making in the work and life of the school and its community.

- Pupils contribute valuably to the Reading Buddies project and Mentor for a Newcomer scheme.

- Pupils have devised and created a time capsule to mark the inauguration of a community building project.

- Pupils worked with a national association to produce a plan for the rehabilitation of a local run-down area.

How well do learners develop skills that will contribute to their future economic well-being?

Inspectors should evaluate how well learners:

- develop their basic skills in literacy, numeracy and ICT

- develop their self-confidence and capacity to work in teams

- become enterprising, able to take initiative and able to recognise the risks involved when making decisions.

This comment represents a good inspection grading:

Most learners are making good progress in literacy, numeracy and ICT. They take the opportunity presented in aspects of learning to operate well in teams and to develop team-working skills. There they often show initiative and a readiness to lead and take responsibility in a sensible way. Their involvement in extracurricular activities and events linked to the wider community is helping them to understand the process of decision-making and to manage responsibility. They are developing the ability to reflect on their decision-making and to review and learn from experience. They are beginning to acquire elements of financial literacy through involvement in school charitable events.

Measures taken by schools

- Years 5 and 6 pupils are getting extensive opportunities to develop creative ICT skills. They have made a narrative film for younger children and an animation. They are developing skills in Power Point for presenting project work.

■ Children are using e-mail to communicate with schools in contrasting geographical locations.

■ Pupils have shared responsibilities for the costing of educational outings.

■ Year 4 pupils have raised funds for class projects through 'assembly line' ventures: the manufacture of greetings cards and bookmarks.

Staying safe

Inspectors will evaluate:

■ whether the requirements of Child Protection legislation are being comprehensively and effectively provided for

■ whether a Child Protection Register and Child Abuse Audit are being maintained and acted on

■ the effectiveness of anti-bullying and anti-racist systems

■ the quality of personal, social and health education (PSHE) and its effectiveness in supporting children's protection and safety

■ provision for children's emotional and social development

■ the quality and effectiveness of health and safety provision and measures

■ the education of children in relation to self-protection and their capacity to guard against any forms of abuse

■ the effectiveness of links with organisations, providers and services involved in pupils' well-being.

This comment represents a good inspection grading:

The safe and supportive environment helps to make children safety conscious and capable of self-protection, without being fearful or inhibited. They are encouraged to develop independence through a stimulating, challenging and well-resourced curriculum and environment.

Health and safety provision is good. A constant check is maintained on all school apparatus, equipment and play provision.

All parents/carers are provided with a written account of the school's policy for the protection and safety of children and suggestions for ways in which school/parents/carers can make active partnerships to this end.

The school collaborates effectively with relevant agencies, groups and societies involved with children's welfare.

Measures taken by schools

- The School Council, with representatives from every age group, makes an important contribution to school ethos and systems designed to reduce and eliminate bullying and to the implementation of effective behaviour-management strategies. The Council provides children with status and a voice.
- The school monitors, records and acts immediately and publicly on all bullying and racist incidents. The governing body is provided with evidence of all recorded incidents and the action taken.
- Pupils are taught about key risks and how to minimise them.
- All out-of-school clubs and activities, whatever their particular focus, place a strong emphasis on bonding, the making of new friendships, mutual support and the engagement of less confident and diffident children.

Chapter 4

Spiritual, moral, social and cultural development

The inspection of spiritual, moral, social and cultural (SMSC) development can be a source of anxiety for many schools, partly because it is such a complex and over-arching area and partly because it is not always clear how it will be evaluated or which criteria are being applied.

Primary schools, with few exceptions, are good places for young people to be: welcoming, cherishing, ordered, stimulating, exciting; where children can mature, learn and achieve, and are happy, secure and celebrated. For some children, especially those growing up in blighted environments and deprived circumstances, schools come to be havens in the fullest sense. So it is understandable that schools should feel confident about the provision they make for spiritual, moral, social and cultural development and expect that others will readily recognise and acknowledge its worth.

Conversely, however, schools often find it easier to explain their work and justify their achievements in literacy and numeracy than they do with spiritual, moral, social and cultural education. Here, generalisations, especially in the areas of spiritual and cultural development, often tend to substitute for evidence of detailed, concrete strategies and implementation.

Spiritual, moral, social and cultural development is central to learners' personal development. The provision for spiritual, moral, social and cultural development has an important bearing on the ECM agenda and on the personal development of learners. Schools recognise and accept this but do not always successfully articulate what they are doing about it.

The following sections offer practical suggestions about the implementation of SCMS development. You are likely to find that some, at least, of what is detailed there is already taking place in your school, but the points raised may help to clarify what is implied by somewhat vague terms such as 'awe and wonder'.

Spiritual development

Young children of course are only at the beginning of what is a life-long process. For them, spiritual awareness and development may well be encapsulated in the useful term 'awe and wonder'. But, whatever it may be, and however difficult it may be to define it, spiritual development doesn't just come about by happy chance and good intentions. It has to be extensively provided for.

Schools support spiritual development through the following:

- the provision of an enriched and carefully ordered environment that engages the senses, inspires the imagination and stimulates curiosity, investigation, invention and reflection

- play and drama that encourages children to create, make believe, represent their experience in various ways, assume roles and solve problems

- generous resources of narrative, literature, poetry and non-fiction that extend horizons

- substantial programmes in the creative and expressive arts; in dance, music, art and design, drama.

Moral development

It is tempting when talking about moral education to fall back on a catalogue of rules, rewards and sanctions and an account of how they are organised within a school to create a moral climate.

But moral education is more than that. Schools, at their best, establish civilised, secure environments based on just, wise, transparent and caring moral codes. It might not seem like this halfway through a wet Wednesday lunchtime – but they do! They are the framework of a good society within which young people grow to be virtuous, moral, compassionate adults. Moral awareness is more than an acceptance of the need to obey rules or to understand the difference between right and wrong. It is an appreciation of the true nature and purpose of a moral code, its principles and values, and a readiness to live according to it in one's own interests and the interests of others and the wider community.

Schools create a sound moral climate through the following:

■ the creation of a clear moral code which is then translated into rules of behaviour that are understood and accepted by all

■ reference to aspects of the curriculum: religious education, literature, drama, the humanities, to cultivate in pupils a genuine moral understanding as distinct from responses based merely on expectation of reward or fear of sanctions

■ consistent monitoring of the ways in which pupils treat each other and behave towards particular groups and individuals

■ the establishment of appropriate sanctions that are clear and acceptable to pupils and parents

■ encouraging pupils to assume responsibilities and obligations as readily as they are to assert rights

■ a whole-school commitment to support the less capable and less advantaged

■ the promotion of a general respect for the concern, pursuits and interests of others, for their cultures, values and beliefs

■ maintaining close professional contact with outside organisations who share a professional concern for the welfare of pupils.

▨ Social development

Social development is about the capacity to mature as an individual in a way that allows one to make the best of oneself, to relate to others in a positive, responsible and caring way and to contribute creatively to the immediate and larger society.

The school, in partnership with the home, is where social awareness, sensitivity and competence are formed and nurtured.

Social development is closely linked to the moral framework which maintains society and institutions, including schools. It is, at the same time, influenced by cultural awareness and sensitivity of spirit.

Schools provide for social development by doing the following:

■ encouraging pupils to relate positively to each other, to take on responsibility and participate in the life of the school community

■ providing programmes that develop pupils' understanding of citizenship and their relation to it

■ ensuring that the whole range of educational provision is contributing to pupils' developing maturity and self-awareness

■ developing pupils' ability to relate to and interact with a widening range of people

■ helping pupils to develop an understanding of what constitutes appropriate behaviour; helping pupils to acquire and cultivate the skills of conversation: discussion, debate, analysis, reflection and response

■ helping pupils to master skills that will enable them to operate and be comfortable in a range of social contexts

■ helping pupils to appreciate and value their personal qualities, abilities and attributes and their potential for learning and achievement.

Cultural development

Two factors present a challenge to schools seeking to provide for cultural development:

- the difficulty of defining what a cultural tradition is, especially in an ethnically diverse school

- the challenges of providing a worthwhile cross-cultural experience for schools so that genuine insight and rapport are fostered.

The need for schools to develop pupils' openness and sympathy for cultural diversity is ever more important in today's multicultural society.

Rich cultural experience can be an inspirational factor in spiritual development. It enhances pupils' awareness of their own heritage and culture and reinforces concepts of themselves as individuals, and of their communities at large. It enhances pupils' awareness of and respect for the cultures and values of other communities. It encourages a reaching out from individuals and communities to others.

Schools provide for cultural development by doing the following:

- placing constant emphasis on the place of story, literature and poetry in pupils' education

- making music, song and dance from different cultures and countries a part of the school's creative and expressive arts programmes

- displaying collections of art and artefacts from different ages, cultures and traditions; using these to help pupils appreciate the vitality, complexity, beauty and significance of human creativity in all times and places

- using history, geography, art and design to help pupils to recognise, understand and appreciate people's cultures, music, literature, song and dance through the ages

- inviting artists, performers and story tellers from other cultures to contribute to school events and celebrations

- using the occasion of educational visits abroad to promote pupils' cultural awareness

- making links with schools with ethnically diverse intakes and a wide cultural tradition.

There will be more items, particular to your school, that you will wish to add. It may be helpful now to look back through each area in the last two chapters and clarify your grasp of the 'Every Child Matters' framework and spiritual, moral, social and cultural development. Then, ask yourself, 'What do we do?' within each of the headings:

- 'How can I find evidence for this?'

- 'Where I can't find it, how can I secure it?' For instance, if you think your school provides worthwhile playtime activities, can you secure this judgement by asking staff views, or inviting a Governor to observe provision?

Remember – be clear what the inspectors are looking for and YOU can provide it. The new relationship works like that. That's what makes it a better way of judging schools.

Chapter 5
The Foundation Stage

This chapter considers:

- some of the guiding principles of early years education
- the rationale of the Foundation Stage
- the challenge of integrating the Reception phase within the whole stage
- the provision for learning activities

Teachers of children in the Early Years need:

- a profound knowledge of child development and the ways in which they learn
- the ability to observe intently children's play and behaviour, to plan action for learning from that observation, and to know when to intervene to take that learning forward
- to be methodical, inventive, knowledgeable and creative in planning learning opportunities
- to integrate successfully the Nursery and Reception Stage into a Foundation Stage. This involves creating learning environments and making curriculum provision for age groups that can extend over a three-year period and an even longer developmental continuum. The pressure felt by some teachers to 'prepare'

Reception Stage children for entry to Key Stage 1, the National Curriculum and eventually formal tests, exacerbates this challenge.

Inspectors pay particular attention to the effectiveness and quality of the Foundation Stage: organisation and management, resource provision, teaching and learning, the record keeping and planning cycle, the impact of the Foundation Stage Profile and *The Curriculum Guidance for the Foundation Stage* (DfES/QCA) and the vital continuity and progression between Nursery and Reception.

The following key points itemise the things a school should be able to identify for an inspection at the Foundation Stage.

■ Curriculum

Ensure that children:

- have access to a broad, rich, balanced curriculum
- are enabled to develop as independent learners in a secure, stimulating and challenging environment, both indoors and outdoors
- are taught by qualified staff proficient and informed about children's early learning and development.

Inform staff about *The Curriculum Guidance for the Foundation Stage*, including 'stepping stones' and the early learning goals, and the implications of these for the children's learning and development.

Ensure provision underpins the six areas of learning.

■ Environment

Develop an environment, both indoors and out, that is stimulating and engaging. Check that it is:

- safe

- very well equipped and maintained

- organised to ensure that children's individual needs are met and that different stages of development are provided for

- attractive and welcoming to visitors and reflects the local and wider community.

Use interesting and innovative displays related to the six areas of learning to encourage interaction, stimulate curiosity and support children's learning.

School ethos

The whole school will have formed its ethos and philosophy round the main principles for early years education, which are:

- that all children feel secure, included and valued

- early years experience builds on what children already know and can do

- the curriculum includes carefully planned activity that ensures opportunity for purposeful teaching and learning within the whole environment

- the children have opportunities to be involved in learning activities planned by adults and activities decided upon and planned by themselves

- the children are provided with time and resources that enable them to be absorbed in what they do, to work in depth and to complete what they set out to do

- the learning environment revolves round carefully planned and purposeful activity. Staff observe and evaluate carefully and intervene sensitively and appropriately to engage children further in the learning process and help them to make progress in their learning.

In translating principles into practice, the school strives to implement *The Curriculum Guidance for the Foundation Stage* by doing the following:

- ■ creating a rich and stimulating learning environment both indoors and outdoors, based around the six areas of learning

- ■ providing carefully selected, interesting, good-quality resources and materials that attract children, appeal to their imagination and encourage them to initiate their own learning

- ■ providing resources and materials that help children to draw on what they already know and can do

- ■ making creative use of outdoor space so that children can work and play on a larger scale

- ■ ensuring that staff are able to spend the major part of their time engaging with the children and their learning

- ■ talking with children and helping them to see the purpose and the possibilities of what they are doing

- ■ planning and using the whole environment and resources to enlarge children's vocabulary and language

- ■ structuring learning activities so they provide as far as possible for the different ways in which children learn and enable children to revisit learning objectives frequently

- ■ providing a judicious mix of adult/learner-planned activities, and offering opportunities for children to work in depth.

The school's planning and assessment cycle will be based on detailed observation and written records of children's use of and response to provision, and the evidence that is gained from that about their learning. Arising from that, the staff make evaluations of individual children's learning and the implications for provision and staff deployment. This, in turn, leads to detailed planning and implementation and back into the cycle of observation and assessment.

The school provides the following areas of provision to support the six areas of learning and to ensure that children have wide opportunity to acquire knowledge and skills:

- home corner with opportunity for fantasy and role play

- creative area and inventive area

- waterworld

- book area

- making and modelling and building in big and small

- ICT area

- music-making area

- mathematics workshop

- exploration, investigation, and discovery area

- art and graphics area.

All areas are generously resourced, carefully organised and clearly and helpfully labelled to ensure that children have easy access to engaging and challenging materials that encourage a wide range of learning. All zones contribute to development in the different areas of learning. Displays in the zones relate to an area of learning; they encourage interaction and curiosity, provide answers, extend awareness and promote language.

The areas of provision are reviewed and planned for on a daily basis; they are monitored and evaluated in relation to their impact on children's activity and learning.

Children are encouraged to take the resources and materials (labelled with names, symbols and pictures) they need for their business and to return them when they are no longer required. This contributes to their growing sense of independence and autonomy.

■ The routine of the day

Resources/activities are organised and available throughout the whole environment so that children can select what they want to do and begin as soon as they arrive.

Children are trained to join with staff in tidying up, returning and re-organising materials and equipment at the end of each session. Apart from ensuring a smooth routine and efficient use of time, this again helps children to be autonomous, responsible and independent.

Children are organised into groups of varying size for story time. Stories are carefully selected and presented to meet the varying needs and development of different groups. Story times are timetabled for the end of sessions to ensure that children have as much time as possible for uninterrupted play and activity.

Playtimes and activities such as PE are also timetabled to ensure minimum interruption to the smooth flow of activities.

Activities are organised so that children can be active and involved until they are collected at the end of sessions.

■ Review

Perhaps the most important points to start with when thinking, discussing and planning with colleagues for teaching and learning in the Early Years are:

- the learning/developmental stages that young children progress through. The definitive guide to turn to here is *Curriculum Guidance for the Foundation Stage* (DfES/QCA 05/00), which defines stepping stones and learning goals and the 'Foundation Stage Profile'

- the range, relevance, quality and learning potential of provision in the setting

- the management of the observation and planning cycle

- the detailed recording of children's progress

■ how you are going to translate the theory and philosophy of education in the early years into practical activity. What exactly are the children going to do on 'a wet Monday morning?'

When we think of the learning styles of very young children, the expectation of freedom to do what they enjoy without being curtailed that they bring from home to a very different kind of setting, and their apparent relatively limited concentration span, then the need for minutely planned and organised activities is clear.

Value what you learn from your observation of children. Look above all for the quality of their absorption in tasks. If this is prolonged and intense, then you are getting a great deal right.

Further reading

Early Years professionals will find the following literature very supportive of good management, curriculum and provision:

■ The essential *Curriculum Guidance for the Foundation Stage* (DfES/QCA, 2005).

■ *A Place to Learn*, written by the Borough of Lewisham Early Years Team and published by Featherstone Education (ISBN 090 1637 10 6). This offers invaluable guidance on the organisation of a Foundation Stage setting.

■ *First hand: Making the Foundation Curriculum Work*, by Sally Featherstone (ISBN 1 902233 54 9)

■ The practical and creative series: *Little Books – with Big Ideas*, published by Featherstone Education. These include *Outdoor Play, Investigations, ICT in the Early Years, Living Things, Science Through Art* and *Cooking Together* (see www.featherstone.uk.com for details).

Chapter 6
Main judgements

The overall judgement on the effectiveness of the school will be formed by judgements on:

- achievement and standards

- personal development and well-being

- quality of provision:
    - teaching and learning
    - curriculum
    - assessment

- leadership and management.

Of course, standards of attainment, and pupil progress are vitally important and inspectors will look for evidence that these improve, reach targets, compare well with schools of similar kind and demonstrate value added for learners. But that is only part of the story. All the things you do as a school that are represented in your SEF are of very great importance. They are what makes a school and shapes the attainment and progress.

Achievement and standards

Inspectors will evaluate:

- the standards reached by learners

- how well learners make progress, taking account of any significant variations between groups of learners

- how well learners with learning difficulties and disabilities make progress.

Inspectors will evaluate the kind of attainment matters listed on pages 17 and 18, using SATs outcomes, PANDA (Performance and Assessment) criteria and LEA data that indicate:

- trends in attainment

- any notable performance by particular groups or cohorts

- attainment, progress and development by pupils with SEN and whether the majority or all of relevant pupils meet IEP targets

- raised attainment/progress on the part of targeted groups

- in some cases, disparity in standards of attainment between long-established pupils in school and later entrants, (especially those who are 'socially mobile') where this illustrates the capacity of the school to add value to pupil performances when afforded sufficient time to do so.

This means that the baseline performance evidence at different stages, e.g. Foundation Stage, end of Key Stage 1, and varying dates of entry to school, etc., is critically important since it is from this that conclusions can be drawn about progress made by school and pupils and, even more important, the value added in terms of pupil performance across key stages.

What schools now seem to do less frequently, in providing evidence about standards and attainment and how well learners achieve, is to refer to pupils' attainment in work that is not evaluated by standardised measures. That represents, in fact, the main body of pupils' work in school. It is the pupils' 'output' and effort, day by day and week by week, that teachers assess, mark and quantify according to quite clearly defined criteria and objectives. The systematic and increasingly sophisticated use of formative assessment over the past couple of decades has provided teachers with prolific and reliable evidence of pupils' attainment and progress, individually and collectively, across the curriculum, as well as enabling them to plan for subsequent work. This evidence on attainment, progress and value added, manifest in pupils' daily work, is at least as valid as outcomes measured in standardised terms.

Consider very carefully how such important evidence can be usefully presented for inspection scrutiny and how representative samples of work could be put forward. This 'everyday' work provides teachers with the substance that enables them to evaluate pupils' attainment and progress and, as a result, set their work for the future and decide on appropriate targets for them. Teachers don't just wait for standardised tests, at the end of term, year or stage, to make decisions about pupils' capability and the learning they should be involved in. In the time now available to inspectors, the opportunity to scrutinise work to anything like the same extent as previously simply does not exist. Indeed, it was one of the great challenges of past inspection: to give to the scrutiny of pupils' work the time that it deserved.

It is up to the schools to find ways of presenting the important evidence of pupils' attainment and progress and the value added to their achievement to be found in their work across the whole curriculum.

Other evidence that Inspectors could refer to includes:

- the data obtained from tracking processes used to monitor learner attainment and progress, to help set targets, to measure value added

- how data provided by years 3–5 QCA, NFER and other tests is used to monitor attainment and progress of individuals, specific groups and year groups; to set targets and predict improvement; to provide information that enables teachers to identify and monitor target groups

- the use of evidence of differential achievement according to gender, ethnic background or other grouping to determine appropriate action on the part of the school

- comprehensive use of the Foundation Stage Profile as a basis for the planning of teaching and learning in the Early Years, for the organisation of curriculum programmes, and for monitoring the children's attainment and progress

- improvements in standards of reading and writing, together with specific teaching and learning strategies and approaches instrumental to bringing this about

- evidence of pupils' attainment and progress in the Foundation Subjects

- evidence of pupils' attainment and progress in ICT

- aspects of pupils' work, attainment and progress targeted for improvement, and the measures put in place to bring this about and criteria for improvement.

Achievement and standards – components of effective provision and practice

- Teaching throughout the school that is consistently focused on the attainment and progress of pupils.

- A curriculum designed to promote pupils' attainment, achievement and progress.

- An effective procedure for promoting educational inclusion and for ensuring that all learners have equal opportunity to achieve; this is underpinned by comprehensive provision for special educational needs.

- The ECM ('Every Child Matters') agenda is implemented and evaluated.

- A programme for continuing professional development that provides appropriately for all teachers in relation to individual needs and experience within the framework of a model of institutional growth and progress.

■ A system of leadership and management designed to enable all staff to contribute to the fullest extent, in line with designated responsibilities, to the realisation of the school's overarching vision, its development/improvement plan and its long-term strategy.

■ The identification of barriers and impediments to pupils' learning and strategies devised for dealing with them.

■ Provision for the consistent monitoring of teaching, concentrated on its relationship to pupils' learning, on the impact it has on their attainment and progress. That the evidence obtained from monitoring is acted upon.

The Performance and Assessment (PANDA) report is a vital tool for all those involved in evaluating or inspecting a school. In order to determine the true nature of the value added by a school, the new PANDA uses a contextual value-added model.

The new PANDA moves away from the use of benchmarks, although it continues to present a wide range of contextual information about a school. The key new developments are:

■ statistical significance tests to assess whether attainment or progress is significantly different from the national average

■ results from the contextual value-added (CVA) model to assess progress made by all pupils, and by groups of pupil, in a school

■ a graph showing each pupil's progress.

The conceptual value-added model involves looking at the progress observed among all pupils nationally in each year, according to a wide range of contextual factors. The main factors in the models include:

■ prior attainment

■ SEN status

- free school meals entitlement

- whether English is an additional language

- ethnicity

- gender

- age

- mobility

- economic deprivation.

Each pupil's expected progress from an earlier Key Stage is calculated, taking into account the national data for all factors in the model. Then their actual progress is compared to their expected progress. The difference indicates whether a pupil has progressed more or less than expected and by how much. These differences are then combined for all pupils to provide a contextual value-added score for each school.

There is no doubt that outright attainment and value-added results will be crucial in inspectors' final judgements. But, as the inspection schedule makes clear, other aspects of school life retain their importance. They include the 'Every Child Matters' agenda; provision for the implementation of the National Curriculum and the Primary Strategy with its aspirations for 'Excellence and Enjoyment', the promotion of spiritual, moral, social and cultural values, together with the development of citizenship, the drive for inclusion, and the ability of a school to make improvement.

If anything, we are in an enlightened time now where schools low on the league tables can riposte most effectively and convincingly to simplistic findings with positive Ofsted reports that take account of the wider educational picture.

Catch your PANDA

DON'T PANIC! A few thoughts . . .

■ In all the emphasis on standardised outcomes, let us not forget that pupils' written and other work are still important in terms of consideration of attainment and progress. A school can and should use such work to demonstrate how good teaching, consistent, constructive formative assessment, creative and effective feedback and challenging targets are contributing to significant attainment and progression on the part of pupils. In this respect, it is instructive for inspectors if samples of pupils' work selected for scrutiny are levelled and graded.

- Use a proven and authoritative system for the purpose of tracking pupils' progress and attainment and for successful target setting.

- Create a special and important post for the management of all aspects of assessment. Ensure that the post holder possesses a comprehensive understanding of the data involved, its statistical significance and the important messages it is offering to the school. Where necessary, support the post holder with expert external analysis and commentary. This person needs time to prepare and answer questions and provide information during an inspection.

- Ensure that the data the school collects and the data provided externally is accurate and correct.

- Investigate data thoroughly for evidence of progress, no matter how negative the overall profile of school achievement may seem. There are likely to be areas/particular groups/cohorts/clusters of pupils where progress and attainment, however slight, are beginning to show. These may offer encouraging evidence of particular strategies and measures having a positive impact, however tentative, and offering encouragement for development.

- Present your evidence on standards and progress in your SEF in as clear and informative a way as possible. Make the most of it all.

Like the real pandas, Chi Chi and Cha Cha, attainment PANDAs can also be uncooperative. Some schools need to provide their own data. For example, a low percentage of level 4+ at Year 6 tests is just one figure about a cohort. If that same cohort had seen a high level of turnover, it could be that pupils who stayed at the school from years 3-6 did much better as a sub-cohort. This sort of data can turn an E* into an A* on the school's 'Independent PANDA'.

Remember you are in charge of this data; it means more to you, has more meaning for you than an external assessor. Inspectors will have mastered the crucial issues in the data but no one will be more familiar with all the implications than you. Highlight them, clarify them, emphasise them in the best interests of the school.

You can find model guidance for presentation of attainment data on the David Fulton website by visiting www.fultonpublishers.co.uk

Acknowledgements

The author is grateful to Ms Elizabeth Hawkins and staff of the Holy Trinity C of E Primary School, Northwood, and the Hertfordshire Intensifying Support Programme Team: Geraldine Louch, School Effectiveness Advisor, Local Authority Inspector Jackie Ashley, Marcus Cooper and Kathryn Little for the use of this model, which they created, and for their advice in relation to attainment monitoring in general.

Personal development and well-being

How good is the personal development and well-being of the learners? In making their judgements here, inspectors will evaluate:

- the extent of learners' spiritual, moral, social and cultural development

- the behaviour of learners

- how well learners enjoy their education

- the extent to which learners adopt safe practices

- the extent to which learners adopt healthy lifestyles

- the extent to which learners make a positive contribution to the community.

This aspect of children's education has always been a matter of the greatest concern for primary schools. However, at times in the past, they might have been hard pressed to define precisely what they did to bring about children's personal development or even exactly what it was they did to guarantee their well-being. That rather vague, well-intentioned approach has been unkindly described as 'cuddle and muddle'. It is unlikely that such a jibe would be justified anywhere today.

Schools need to provide clear statements evaluating their provision in this area.

The following are examples of such provision:

- The children develop a sense of self-worth through many opportunities to contribute to the life of the school and community. Activities include membership of the School Council, opportunity to host visitors, helping to run after-school clubs and activities.

- The school uses a range of strategies to identify and support children who feel at risk.

- A module of the PSHE programme helps children to deal constructively with their emotions and to relate well to others.

- Formative assessment, interactive marking and constructive feedback to pupils provide recognition of attainment and progress and enhance self-esteem.

Quality of provision

The quality of provision includes:

- teaching and learning
- curriculum
- assessment.

These areas are at the heart of a school and make it what it is.

Showing the best of teaching

Learning is the central function of the school. Here, more than anywhere else, we need to be ready for inspection. So what are the inspectors looking for? Drawing on inspection criteria, the following sections provide outlines of some crucial facets the school should be able to demonstrate and offer a checklist for evaluation or prompt sheet for development.

Learning

The inspection will want to know about the following features and characteristics of pupils' learning. They will want to know how pupils:

- acquire new knowledge and skills, develop their ideas, increase their understanding

- show engagement, application and concentration and are productive

- develop the skills and capacity to work independently and collaboratively

- understand how well they are doing and how to improve

- acquire language in its various forms as a main influence on learning and understanding

- draw on the physical, intellectual, emotional and social aspects of development

- use mistakes and misconceptions (learning from 'negative knowledge' is an important part of the learning process)

- engage with learning in the three main ways: auditory, visual and kinaesthetic. Almost all learners use all three modes, though about a quarter may have a strong bias to one style only. Teachers take broad account of this in planning for children's learning

- how far EAL learners are supported by appropriate resources, including bilingual materials; grouping for learning; opportunity to use first language with staff and response partners, the use of resources and ICT aimed at acceleration of language acquisition.

The following prompts for the evaluation of teaching may be helpful in relation to leadership and management.

Subject knowledge

Teachers will demonstrate a good command of subjects, programmes of study and areas of learning by:

■ planning and implementing lessons that serve the learning needs of pupils across the whole ability range

■ helping learners to make links with other subjects

■ inspiring learners' interest, enthusiasm and curiosity about the subject.

Challenging learning

Teachers engage, stimulate and challenge pupils by:

■ providing lively and interesting learning experiences

■ creating or inviting problems that stimulate speculation, imagination, investigation and invention

■ teaching learners strategies for problem-solving

■ encouraging pupils' creativity

■ presenting lively, well-paced lessons, while at the same time allowing for discussion, reflection and revisiting

■ the effective use of ICT and high-quality software.

A learning environment

Teachers create an environment that supports good teaching and learning through:

■ inventive, inviting, interactive displays over a wide curriculum and cultural range that extend pupils' subject knowledge and stimulate eagerness to discover and know more

■ the efficient organisation of good-quality resources, materials and equipment to which learners have easy access and for the managing of which they have some responsibility

- the flexible organisation of furniture to allow for varying learning activities

- a language-rich environment

- displays of work that celebrate attainment/achievement and provide annotated models of what pupils should aim for

- provision for small group and independent learning

- access to high-quality literature and non-fiction.

Purposeful planning

Teachers plan effectively by:

- setting clear, worthwhile learning objectives, designed to help pupils attain, make progress and widen their understanding. They build on pupils' previous learning and understanding and on the information gained from systematic formative assessment

- building in provision for pupils' varied learning needs and for those whose progress within the lessons calls for more challenging work

- closely relating lesson planning to National Curriculum programmes

- planning that incorporates success criteria aimed at mapping pupils' attainment and progress

- involving learning assistants in the planning. The planning details their work with pupils, clarifies its place in the whole-class learning programme and emphasises the learning objectives implicit in the activity as distinct from merely aiming at conclusion of assignments

- setting up tasks, designed and systematically applied to assess pupils' attainment and progress

- ensuring that published materials and commercial resources used are of good quality, relevant and guaranteed to make a substantial contribution to pupils' learning

- taking account of future learning.

Good behaviour

Teachers effectively manage behaviour through the following measures:

- The ethos and climate of the classroom make pupils feel secure, assured, and confident about learning.

- The classroom environment is stimulating, challenging and supportive of pupils' learning.

- The classroom is well organised and resourced, and is efficiently managed by staff and pupils.

- Teaching is planned and carried out to meet the full range of pupils' needs.

- Tasks are precisely differentiated to support SEN learners.

- Pupils have had a say in the framing of rules for class behaviour. They understand the rationale that underpins the rules and the consequences of breaking them. They accept the rules as fair and respect the authority of the teacher and support staff.

- Careful provision is made to ensure that all pupils achieve genuine success and are involved in evaluating personal progress and target setting.

- Sanctions for misbehaviour are clear, fair, transparent, carried through and designed to support improvement.

- The classroom is an inclusive environment where all individuals, and cultural and social diversity, are respected.

Classroom management

Lesson management strongly supports pupils' learning, as follows:

- Learning assistants are engaged in lesson planning and are informed about IEPs and EAL language levels.

- Learning assistants, informed, well trained and creatively directed, provide strong support for pupils' learning, particularly with groups and individuals.

- Learning objectives are presented to pupils visually and orally; the learning they will bring about is clarified; the distinction between activities and the learning they will bring about is understood by the children.

- Lessons begin punctually, open in an engaging and interesting way, stimulate learners' curiosity and encourage participation.

- Questioning is pointed, differentiated and supportive and advances pupils' learning.

- The teachers' exposition is clear, is supported by imaginative and relevant use of visual materials, including, where appropriate, ICT and generally occupies no more than a third of the total lesson time.

- The pace of the lesson is carefully managed, with lively and brisk presentation but with opportunity for learners to think and reflect, to share views with partners, to air their views and to seek clarification where necessary.

- Pupils' assignments are carefully prepared and differentiated to ensure individual pupil attainment and progress; teacher and learning assistant ensure monitoring of assignments.

- Assignments are interesting, engaging, well matched and challenging.

- Provision is made for pupils whose progress calls for further challenge.

- Opportunity is built into sufficient lessons for recorded formative assessment.

- The interactive plenary session helps pupils to identify their learning and what has helped them to achieve it, what aspects need improvement or could be improved, and what learning is likely to come next.

A curriculum related to its learners

In making judgements here, inspectors will evaluate:

- the extent to which the curriculum or activities match learners' needs, aspirations and capabilities, building on prior attainment and experience

- the extent to which the provision enables and encourages learners to be healthy and stay safe

- how far the curriculum meets external requirements and is responsive to local circumstances

- the extent to which enrichment activities and, where appropriate, extended services contribute to learners' enjoyment and achievement.

Prioritisation of literacy and numeracy

Literacy and numeracy are priorities for learning and gain from:

- daily/regular provision for both subjects

- highly focused provision through the Foundation Stage underpinned by a wide, experientially rich curriculum, first-hand experience and opportunity for children to work in small groups with adults expert in Early Years provision

- clear rationale for the place of phonics and spelling.

The following exemplar from a school represents an effective approach to the teaching of literacy:

- Major emphasis on provision for the achievement of the Early Learning Goals for Communication, Language and Literacy in the Foundation Stage. A member of the senior management team, largely free of designated teaching commitment, has been appointed to coordinate on a full-time basis the work of the Foundation Stage. A large-scale building project has provided purpose-built accommodation for the whole phase, enhancing continuity between the Nursery and Reception. Staff training and the provision of resources have provided strong support for the promotion of the literacy goals: language for communication and for thinking; for linking sounds and letters; for reading, handwriting and writing.

- There is a well-established home–school reading partnership backed by story sacks, games, engaging literacy investigation cards and user-friendly guidelines made available to parents.

■ A whole-school policy for the provision of narrative is implemented daily across the whole school.

■ The school writing policy is underpinned by a rich and stimulating whole-school learning environment, wide narrative experience; extensive and constantly updated non-fiction resources, video material and interactive technology.

■ The school science policy has been revised, adapted and resourced, with an increased time allocation to ensure that pupils have more opportunity to participate in investigation, 'detection' and experimental work.

Assessment *for* learning and assessment *of* learning

Effective assessment contributes powerfully to pupils' confidence, self-esteem and motivation, qualities that are essential if pupils are to learn successfully and make satisfactory progress.

We should think of assessment from two perspectives:

■ assessment *of* learning

■ assessment *for* learning.

Assessment of learning is known as *summative assessment*. It is concerned with judging pupils' performance against national standards. Summative assessments are judgements made at the conclusion of units of work, at the end of Key Stages, the end of terms or the end of years. In summative assessment, test results are increasingly expressed in levels to describe pupils' performance.

Assessment for learning is known as *formative assessment*. In other words, it is an assessment used to form or shape learning. However, formative assessments uses summative data for formative purposes, that is, to shape and modify pupils' learning. Assessment for learning is the use of assessments in the classroom to raise pupils' attainment and achievement and to help them make satisfactory progress. If pupils are to improve their performance as far as possible, teachers need to understand that assessment for learning plays a crucial role in revising pupils' standards of attainment and in supporting their progress.

Assessment is relevant to every subject. Schools need to be able to demonstrate for inspection that:

■ They have in place an effective policy for assessment for learning.

■ The policy is working in relation to pupils' learning.

■ That assessment for learning is helping to raise learners' standards of attainment and is supporting their progress.

Obviously, there will be more assessment of writing than of knowledge of major rivers, for instance. Good assessment practice must be balanced with the priorities of the school. Some assessment involves gathering and reviewing data – some can be covered by an effective marking policy. See PANDA discussion on pages 62–65.

Leadership and management

What is the overall effectiveness and efficiency of leadership and management? In guidance to inspectors about the evaluation of leadership and management, it is stressed they should take account of their impact in terms of the outcomes for learners and the quality of provision.

In making their judgements, inspectors will evaluate:

■ how effectively leaders and managers at all levels set clear direction, leading to improvement, and promote high-quality care and education

■ how effectively performance is monitored and improved through quality assurance and self-assessment

■ how well equality of opportunity is promoted and discrimination tackled so that all learners achieve their potential (i.e. inclusion)

■ the adequacy and suitability of staff, including the effectiveness of processes for recruitment and selection of staff to ensure that learners are well taught and protected

■ the adequacy and suitability of staff, specialist equipment, including ICT, learning resources and accommodation

- how effectively and efficiently resources are deployed to achieve value for money

- whether the leadership and management provide the school with the capacity to make the necessary improvements, as shown in its performance since the last inspection.

Where appropriate, the following will also be assessed:

- how effective are the links made with other providers, services, employers and other organisations to promote the integration of care, education and any extended services to enhance learning

- the extent to which governors and other supervisory boards discharge their responsibilities.

Leadership and management are no longer seen as the responsibility of the head teacher and senior staff alone. It is common to talk about 'dispersed leadership' and 'flat' management structures. What this means is that everyone on a staff must have a very clear understanding of what the school stands for, what it aims to achieve in the interests of its pupils, how it plans to go about achieving that aim, and what the role of the individual member of staff requires them to contribute to the process. Clearly, these roles and contributions will vary significantly. The implementation of workforce reforms has challenged schools to be rigorous, reflective and creative. They have responded effectively to the demand. Present to inspectors the evidence of what you have done in this context in the most informative way possible.

The head teacher, supported by a senior management team, leads the school, frames its philosophy and sense of mission, creates its guiding 'vision' and is responsible and accountable for its management and organisation. The head and her/his senior team are responsible for the quality of work achieved by teachers and pupils, for standards of attainment and progress, for identifying and building on strengths and eradicating weaknesses, for maintaining improvement, for ensuring appropriate value added to pupils' education, and for providing for implementation of systems and the provision of resources to bring these about. They will be expected to have:

- a fully informed and accurate picture of the quality of teaching and learning throughout the school and the impact of teaching on learning success

- a fully informed and accurate picture of how outcomes compare with national and local standards, and whether learner progress is satisfactory or better.

Their perceptions will be based on comprehensive objective evidence and substantial monitoring.

Subject coordinators will carry responsibility for the overall quality of their curriculum area, for monitoring the outcomes of teaching and learning, the levels of achievement and progress, for leading colleagues in planning and review, for contributing to staff development through appropriate INSET programmes. There is sometimes disagreement with professional associations about how far coordinators 'lead' and carry complete responsibility for what is happening in their areas of responsibility. Fortunately, schools seem capable of reaching sensible compromise on the matter.

Class teachers, even those with no designated responsibility outside the care of their particular class – rare indeed in primary schools today – are required to think of themselves as managers of their pupils' learning, using time, resources, efficient class management and organisation and data to the very best extent in carrying out the task.

Another dimension is now added to many class teachers' leadership and management responsibilities through the great increase in learning assistants. Most Nursery teachers over the years, however inexperienced, have been familiar with the often demanding responsibility of forming an effective working relationship with nursery nurses while at the same time being accountable, in ways that were not always explicit or documented, for ensuring they did their work efficiently. Now most teachers are similarly responsible for making an effective working relationship with learning assistants while being very clearly accountable for their performance in working with the pupils.

Governing bodies have important statutory responsibilities. They are accountable to pupils, parents and the wider community for the overall performance and the achievement and progress of the school. They are responsible for curriculum policy, for the making and management of the school improvement/development plan, for monitoring the school's progress, achievement and general effectiveness.

Governors are required to do the following:

■ provide a strategic view of where the school must go

■ hold the school to account for the educational standards it achieves and the quality of education it provides

■ act as an informed and critical friend to the school.

The fortunes of a school, the head teacher and staff and governing bodies are inextricably bound up together; they are accountable to each other. Heads need to use their termly reports to ensure the key messages about the school's development of the 'Every Child Matters' agenda are lodged in Governor's awareness of the school.

Inspectors' judgement about the quality of leadership and management will be greatly influenced by two factors:

■ the school's success in dealing with key issues from the previous inspection

and, of vital importance

■ how far the school is competent to secure improvement in the future.

Leaders, managers and Governors must demonstrate that there is capacity to bring about the improvements that inspection has identified as necessary. They will do this in the following ways:

■ They will have dealt successfully with the key issues for action identified by the previous inspection. Where issues have not been successfully dealt with or completed, the school will be able to provide evidence that the causes of this lay outside their control.

■ The school can demonstrate that the lessons learned from the process of improvement have contributed, where relevant, to the school's achievement and progress in other respects.

■ The school can demonstrate that the action taken has had a significant impact on achievement, attainment, and clear, substantial and sustained progress.

■ The school has in place a strong and effective system of self-evaluation that involves all staff and pupils and is supported by robust and informed external evaluation.

■ The process of self-evaluation is underpinned by expert and systematic analysis of performance data. The school can demonstrate that it uses the outcomes of data analysis to drive school improvement, help raise performance and enhance value added.

■ The school can show that it does not merely identify areas of weakness but acts effectively to improve them. It is not satisfied with aspiration alone but sets out to achieve tangible improvement.

■ The school implements strong, rigorous and systematic monitoring of standard, performance and the general quality of education.

■ The school is implementing effective strategic planning. There is a detailed, costed, resourced improvement/development plan, with monitored, time-allocated success criteria to which all staff subscribe and are involved in.

■ The school has access to and uses informed and critical external analysis and evaluation.

■ All actions and processes are monitored for demonstrable beneficial effect.

■ Review

Let me conclude by emphasising that what you have read here about leadership and management is a model to aspire to, that no one ever fully achieves. However, if the thinking that underlies it informs your school, then it is likely that you are providing more than satisfactory leadership.

And remember that leadership is 'dispersed,' is shared by many. You are not the only one accountable.

Epilogue

In the book I have recommended that head teachers invite fellow professionals to act, on occasions, as informed critics on aspects of the life and work of their schools. I believe that, as this kind of development becomes more common, augmented by regular light evaluation franchised to bodies such as Institutes of Education and others qualified to judge, the inspection system as we know it, even now, will become largely redundant. Schools will be in the business of commissioning their own external evaluation, because their levels of professional competence will entitle them to do so.

And it may happen sooner than we think. I believe that inspection, common today, will have gone by the time your present new school intake leaves you.

So, inspection? Enjoy it and use it creatively while you can, for the larger benefit of the school and the learners.

INDEX

absorption in tasks, learners' 57
Active Mark award 39
arts education 24
Ashley, Jackie 66
'assembly line' ventures 43
assertion, use of 21
assessment *for* learning and
    assessment *of* learning 74–5
assignments, pupils' 72
Audley Primary School 32

Baker, Neil 32
behaviour management 71
bullying 43–4

challenging learning 69
Chief Inspector of Schools 1–2
child abuse and child protection
    43
child development 51, 56
Children Act (2004) 33
classroom management 71–2
clubs out of school hours 44, 67
contextual value-added (CVA) 2,
    62

continuing professional
    development 61–2
Cooper, Marcus 66
critical friend role 19
cross-cultural experience 49
cultural development of pupils
    49–50
curriculum provision 28–9, 36–7,
    51–4, 72–3; *see also*
    National Curriculum

Department for Education and
    Science (DfES) 17
deputy head teachers 29
development plans of schools 17,
    19, 31, 79
dialogue between schools and
    inspectors 2
disabilities, pupils with 59
dispersed leadership 76, 80
displays of work 53, 69–70
documents needed by inspectors
    11

Early Learning Goals 27

Early Years education 51, 53, 56
e-mail, use of 43
emotional development of pupils
     35, 43
English as an additional language
     (EAL) 3, 68, 71
'enjoying and achieving' 29, 34–5,
     39–40
environments for learning 52–4,
     69–71, 74
equality of opportunity 75
ethnic diversity 49
ethos of a school 53
Every Child Matters (ECM) agenda
     18, 22, 27, 33–44, 45, 50,
     61, 63, 78
evidence forms used by inspectors
     13–14
evidence of pupils' attainment and
     progress 59–61
extended provision by schools 30,
     37

family learning provision 40
'flat' management structures in
     schools 76
formative assessment 3, 60, 67,
     70, 72, 74
Foundation Stage 51–4, 73
Foundation Stage profiles 61
foundation subjects 13, 40

gifted and talented pupils 18
governors of schools 8, 11, 14, 18,
     20, 23, 38, 44, 76, 78
grading scale used by Ofsted 14,
     22

guidance for learners 37

Hawkins, Elizabeth 66
head teachers, personal
     characteristics of 22–3, 29,
     76, 78
healthy lifestyles 38–9

inclusion, educational 61, 71, 75
individual education plans (IEPs)
     11–12, 59
information and communication
     technology (ICT) 3, 24, 40,
     42, 61, 68–9, 72, 75
initial contacts between inspectors
     and schools 6–7
INSET programmes 24, 77
inspection of schools, prospects
     for 81; *see also*
     new inspection system
interactive whiteboards 24, 40

jargon, use of 21
judgements about school
     effectiveness 13–14, 22, 27,
     30, 36, 58, 78

Key Stage 2 assessments 24

leadership of schools 3, 21, 37,
     62, 75–6, 79–80
     as distinct from management
     29–30
league tables 63
learning, features and
     characteristics of 68
learning assistants 70–2, 77

learning difficulties 59
learning styles 57
lesson management 71–2
library provision 24
literacy 3, 40, 42, 73
Little, Kathryn 66
local circumstances 28–9, 37
Louch, Geraldine 66

Mentor a Newcomer scheme 42
minority ethnic groups 18
mistakes, learning from 68
moral development of pupils
    46–7

National Curriculum 27, 52, 63,
    70
new inspection system
    benefits of 2
    critical differences in 5–6
    duties of inspection teams
        10–12
    flexibility and responsiveness in
        12
    scope of evaluations 15
New Relationship With Schools
    (NRWS) 17
notice to improve 14
numeracy 3, 40, 42, 73

objectives of learning 70, 72
observation
    of children's behaviour 51–4,
        57
    of delivery of lessons 7, 13, 28
Office for Standards in Education
    (Ofsted) 3, 10, 14, 34

pacing of lessons 72
parental involvement 24–6, 73
performance and assessment
    (PANDA) reports 2, 9, 20,
        62, 64–5, 75
personal, social and health
    education (PSHE) 43, 67
personal development of pupils
    18, 27, 37, 45, 66
planning by teachers 70
plenary sessions in class 72
policies of individual schools 11
PowerPoint presentations 42
pre-inspection briefings (PIBs)
    9–10
Primary Strategy 63
priorities for improvement 19
programmes and activities,
    educational 36–7

quality of educational provision
    13–14, 36, 67–75

racism 43–4
Reading Buddies project 42
resources for learning 54–6,
    69–70, 76
routine of the school day 56

sanctions for misbehaviour 71
schemes of work 11
school councils 41, 44, 67
school evaluation form (SEF) 7–9,
    19–32, 58, 65
    structure of 23–30
school improvement partners
    (SIPs) 19

science policies of schools 74
self-evaluation by schools 2, 5–6,
    9–13, 16–20, 79
  link with actions 19–20
  scope of 17–18
  see also school evaluation form
senior management teams 76–7
significance tests 62
skills, acquisition of 36, 40, 68
social development of pupils 43,
    48
society, contributions to 41
special educational needs (SEN)
    11–12, 17, 24, 40, 59, 61, 71
special educational needs
    coordinators (SENCOs) 12
special measures 14
spiritual, moral, social and cultural
    (SMSC) development 45–6,
    49, 63
standards 27, 35, 59
story-telling 56
strategic planning in schools 79

subject coordinators 77
subject knowledge, teachers' 69
summative assessment 22, 74
support for learners 37

team-working, pupils' 42
thinking skills 40
Times Educational Supplement
    (TES) 1
timetabling
  of lessons 56
  of school inspections 6–9
tracking of pupils' progress 65
trails' followed by inspections 8–9

value added by schools 2–5, 27,
    58–63, 76
vision 31, 62
visitors' guides to schools 41

weaknesses identified in individual
    schools 21
workforce reforms 76